PENGUIN BOOKS

HOW TO BE A FASCIST

MICHELA MURGIA is an award-winning writer and a political activist. She has written travel books, political nonfiction, and novels, for which she has been awarded the Premio Campiello and the Mondello International Literary Prize.

ALEX VALENTE is an award-winning literary translator and teacher. His current translations into English include *Can You Hear Me?* by Elena Varvello, stories by Natalia Ginzburg and Elsa Morante for The Short Story Project, contributions to the *Italian Literature in Translation* fiction anthology, and the forthcoming *Fidelity* by Marco Missiroli.

T0176199

HOW TO BE A FASCIST

A MANUAL

Michela Murgia
Translated from the Italian by
Alex Valente

PENGUIN BOOKS

PENGUIN BOOKS

An imprint of Penguin Random House LLC

penguinrandomhouse.com

First published in Great Britain by Pushkin Press 2020
Published in Penguin Books 2020

Originally published in Italian as *Istruzioni per diventare fascisti*
by Einaudi editore s.p.a., Turin

LIBRARY OF CONGRESS CATALOGING-IN-PUBLICATION DATA

Names: Murgia, Michela, 1972– author.
Title: How to be a fascist : a manual / Michela Murgia;
translated from the Italian by Alex Valente.
Other titles: Istruzioni per diventare fascisti. English
Description: New York : Penguin Books, 2020.
Identifiers: LCCN 2020011537 (print) | LCCN 2020011538 (ebook) |
ISBN 9780143136057 (trade paperback) | ISBN 9780525507673 (ebook)
Subjects: LCSH: Fascism. | Ideology. | Fascism—Italy.
Classification: LCC JC481 .M82413 2020 (print) |
LCC JC481 (ebook) | DDC 320.53/3—dc23
LC record available at https://lccn.loc.gov/2020011537
LC ebook record available at https://lccn.loc.gov/2020011538

Printed in the United States of America
1   3   5   7   9   10   8   6   4   2

Set in Sabon MT Pro

CONTENTS

For Francesco and Angelica
and it's already too late

HOW
TO BE
A
FASCIST

Necessary methodological premise

write against democracy because it has always been, since its origins, an irredeemably flawed system of government. What Winston Churchill said was false: democracy isn't the worst form of government except for all others—the truth is that it's the worst, full stop, but it's always hard to say it openly, in public, despite all the clear evidence in our daily experiences.

The book you're holding is born from a desire to demonstrate that democracy is not only useless, but in fact toxic to coexistence, and also to prove that its tried and tested opposite—fascism—is a much better system of state administration: less costly, faster, and more efficient. This text aims especially to be a comprehension tool for the more educated classes exhausted by democracy, because it has never been necessary to explain to the masses that fascism is better. Armed with the secret wisdom of the simple mind, the people already know as much, and that is why, tired of the inability of the democratic system to solve their problems, they regularly and almost spontaneously turn toward fascism.

I say *almost* not by chance, because at times fascism may need some help to take root; at the beginning of their historical cycle, democracies tend to be quite hostile toward it and attempt to organize themselves against it with blatantly crude methods, such as passing laws to make it illegal. Fascism, fortunately, knows how to wait. It's like herpes— primary organisms are always the ones that teach us the most—able to survive for entire decades within the marrow of democracy, letting everyone believe it has disappeared, only then to pop out, more viral than ever, at the first, entirely predictable weakening of its immune system.

A young democracy, especially one born out of a war or a civil revolution, will be quick to react to fascism, but an older one will have lost most of its memory and will have buried the eyewitnesses who supported its rhetoric. Additionally, it will have faded and be sufficiently corrupted to consider compromises on its principles, increasingly more significant, with other forms of government. At that point, if fascism is quick and able to seize the opportunity, it will be able to rule entire states without ever picking up a single weapon: it will be democracy's own tools that will allow it to establish itself, and finally prevail.

At this exact moment in history, we have at our disposal an overabundance of tools of mass control that no fascism from the past century ever had, and this allows us to attempt something new: to rise from the heart of an aging democratic system and dominate it without ever making use of military force, internal or external. By manipulating the tools of democracy, we can make an entire country fascist without ever even mentioning the word *fascism*, which might still raise some resistance, even in a faded democracy. Rather, we should ensure that fascist language is socially accepted in all spheres of communication, suitable for any topic, like an unlabeled can—not left, not right—that can be passed from hand to hand without anyone ever touching its contents.

Contents. This is the crucial issue. I can't hide the fact that yes, they are problematic, and we won't, at least at the beginning, make them pass unchallenged in a democracy. We no longer live in a time when we can explicitly affirm the superiority of one race over others, or openly say that not all opinions have the right to be expressed, especially if they go against the national interest. You can think it, of course, and even say it in certain circumstances, but to present oneself as a system that openly states it as a political manifesto can be difficult at the outset. For this reason, you will not find in these pages anything that might define "fascist ideas." Trying to affirm fascism at the level of ideas is a long process, too complex and contradictory to be worth the attempt. Too many years of rhetoric. Too many remembrance days. Too much ideological fluff about the Allied efforts that ensured that everyone remembers their veteran grandad and no one ever remembers the fascist one. Looking into the merit of these ideas isn't productive; if, instead, we act on the method, the ideas will simply follow.

When it comes to politics, method and contents coincide, and the fascist method holds the power of alchemical transmutation: if applied without any ideological prejudice, it turns whoever makes use of it into a fascist, because—as Forrest Gump would say—fascist is as fascist does. What follows, then, is a manual on the method—specifically, instructions on the language, the most malleable cultural infrastructure we have. Why would anyone need to overthrow institutions if all you need to do in order to seize them is to change the referent of a word, and make sure everyone speaks it? Words generate behavior, and those who control words control behavior. That's the starting point: the names we give to things and the way we talk about them. That's where fascism can face the challenge of becoming current again. If every day we can convince even a single person who believes in democracy, we can live again. And live greatly.

Faithful to its humble didactic aim, this book includes as an appendix a short test of the understanding reached through reading, and an evaluation of the progress made in adhering to fascism.

Head-first

To become a fascist, the first post you need to plant is the word *leader*, as currently understood by democratic systems. No democracy, in the pursuit of the utopia of all being equal, has ever been able to avoid the contradiction of having to organize its equality through hierarchies. Even those who believe in democracy know that a guiding hand is necessary, but they expect to elect it and control it through so much red tape and bureaucracy that, ultimately, the person supposed to lead them ends up being the least powerful. Democracy has taken hold of the promising concept of *guiding* behind the word *leader*—*führer* in German—and watered down its nature to fit its own agenda. And so what would have been a charismatic figurehead has ended up taking the shape of a spineless temporary representative, subject to every electoral wind and forced to endure the shame of having to be voted for, not only during elections, but also within their own political community. These idiotic consultations are called "primaries" or "leadership races," but what emerges from them is always secondary, as the power of mass voting is too changeable: today you have their approval, tomorrow you don't. This makes everything unstable, and unstable government is the first of democracy's flaws.

What is the linguistic alternative that fascism can offer to the confused and bland concept of the *leader*? Easy: *head*. It's not a matter of changing the word: we can happily keep calling them *leaders*, as long as the difference between the two is made clear. A *leader* inspires and points out a direction, but— due to democracy—pays the not insignificant price of having people not necessarily follow it. And if people convince themselves that they can't go in a certain direction, you can rest assured that they will not. A leader who can be contested has no real power. A real head, on the other hand, never compromises. He dictates a direction and personally takes the first step, showing himself capable of conquering something that is always just ahead of where his followers can see. Inspiration is great, sure, but it's the stuff of poets, not politicians: to run a country, you need someone decisive in his actions and without hesitation in dragging his followers with him, obliterating any obstacle with all the tools at his disposal.

The problem with a democratic leader is that they engage with differences in opinion and give them equal weight, so that—just when a decision needs to be taken—it is delegitimized by those who disagree. A head is frank, loyal, doesn't pretend to consider the thousand objections that arise around any person in power, and for this reason, his decisions are non-negotiable. When he's in power, he can win or he can lose, but a head must always be obeyed, because those who don't are undermining the possibility of victory. The difference between the spineless democrats and the head is all here: you do not debate with the head, because if he were to waste time debating with those who think differently in a country where everyone believes they could coach an NFL team, no decision would ever be made.

A second advantage of having a head is speed of action. If the person in power has greater decision-making freedom, it guarantees an enormous savings of time when making the necessary choices: the fewer people you need to consult, the sooner you make a decision. The more a democracy is representative of every single political minority, the slower the executive process will be, and this, in turn, will be seen by the people as insufferable inaction. However, in case the people take too long to understand that democratic slowness is to blame for this inefficiency, we must make use of every situation to belittle parliamentarianism, and its forms of representation, and suggest presidentialism, for example, as the more efficient alternative. We will have to pass electoral laws that favor the concentration of votes on a single strong figure to polarize opinions, or at least pit two sides against each other. It is essential that local autonomy be reduced or, even better, removed, so that structural decisions can be taken in a non-confrontational context or at least reduced to the smaller, uninfluential details.

Limiting the opportunities for mass participation (parties, commissions, committees, various councils) will serve to implant the idea that whoever is in power must act with as much freedom as possible or they will never be able to act productively. It can take years, but once the importance of the role of the head is established again, he will act with the same strength that moves us to love heroes and become fans of public figures, rising to be a model not of inspiration ("I want to be *like* him"), but rather aspiration ("I want to *be* him"). For this to happen, it is crucial to insist that all organs of democratic negotiation are useless red-tape dead ends where nothing ever happens. The more people hear this, the sooner it will seem natural that concentrating all power into the hands of a single strong individual, who knows what needs to be done, is the only logical conclusion, and a lot more efficient than having to listen to a weak country's opinions.

Then there is the financial aspect. It's self-evident that having a single man in charge costs much less than having a guide who is constantly forced to consult the guided. That is because democracy has multiple levels of checks and balances between multiple differing positions, and requires these to be simultaneously represented. As well as requiring more time, this also means that multiple representatives need to be paid. The head is cheaper, as he decides alone or with a small group of loyal people. Whether you call it a magic circle of chosen ones, council of the just or "rose of the inner circle," it makes no difference: the fewer people are making the decisions, the fewer we need to pay. If this were the right time to call things by their name, we'd have to recognize that the absolute cheapest form of government is a dictatorship, as only one person gets paid. But we are still far from that level of virtuous administration of resources; being able to appoint a head who makes decisions with a select few would already be a great step forward in cutting our current costs.

Meanwhile, continuing to point out how much a democratic administration is costing us will help set the stage for removing it. Remind everyone how much we pay members of Congress; keep asking for the reduction of their salaries, their entourages, their pensions, and any form of funding to parties; this is a discussion that ensures a consensus, as everyone believes that politicians are paid too much. By insisting on this, even those who believe in democracy will start believing that what is really costing us money is democracy itself.

The biggest advantage, however, of having a head rather than a leader is something else: those in power shape those under their power, starting a process that eventually leads to the two parties becoming similar to one another. A people with a leader will be loud, dissenting; will demand to be heard, to debate decisions they don't like; will try making them lose approval; won't respect authority; will take to the streets and complain; won't be thankful or obedient. The people who choose a head, on the other hand, will be trusting and rely on him, recognizing the superior vision of the one who makes the decisions; they won't constantly interfere, and if they do take to the streets, it will be to support and acclaim the man who generously bears the heavy burden of leadership.

The population that recognizes a head lives better and relies on him, obeying the desire for a master that secretly lives within us all, that tendency toward one whose strength not even Étienne de La Boétie was able to deny when, in the 1500s, he warned people against the risk— as he called it—of dictatorship. In his *Discourse on Voluntary Servitude*, La Boétie argued that every time we address in the singular a social plurality, we are favoring tyranny. If only! The sadder reality is that this is a utopian objective for a contemporary fascist. The days when a *duce*, a king or a tribune could single-handedly rule an entire population are over. The *tendency toward one*, however, can be exploited to

at least limit pluralism and erode democratic institutions, removing as many players from the field as
possible. Once the people have been educated to
recognize themselves in a head, the second step is
to maintain the approval through communication,
making it as efficient and trivial as possible. You
read that right: trivial.

To simplify is too complex

Democracy has the idiotic quality of being a form of government based on dissent rather than consensus: this means, unfortunately, that anyone with an opinion is convinced that everyone else can't wait to hear it. Too many decades of democratic meandering have ruined people, accustoming them to the idea that there can be dissenting opinions even among those in power, and that part of the time used to govern the state should instead be dedicated to constant debate, resulting in understandable inefficiency.

· Not too long ago there was an efficient system for dealing with the chaos generated by this undisciplined pretense: fascism identified the dissidents and silenced them by exiling and isolating them or sending them directly to prison, where no one could hear them; alternatively, it would convince everyone, by force if necessary, that it was better to agree with the head's ideas than constantly to suggest different ones and thereby ultimately interfere with those trying to get the country going.

Unfortunately, the rise of the internet has changed things drastically. Even if we sent someone to a remote island, we'd have at least to ensure that there were no signal or connection, because any on-line space, any social-media page, any live stream removes distances and amplifies voices, making it impossible actually to prevent anyone from speaking. This is definitely a problem, but fascism has never avoided making an opportunity out of a problem, and when chaos cannot be stopped, we must use it to further our goals.

The obstacle that modernity presents to the development of fascism is that everyone—not only the head—has a way of being heard; the best, fascist solution, then, is to let them speak. Always. All of them. At the same time. About everything. Without any hierarchy or authority of opinions. If in the past millions of people used TV and newspapers as reference points, today they spend their entire time on social media, commenting, sharing, liking or disliking, and there is no reason to prevent them from doing so. Because the fact that everyone does it means that each and every voice becomes indistinguishable from the others and, ultimately, irrelevant.

Democracy claims that we're all equal? Let's demonstrate it by making sure all opinions are also seen as equal. If we convince everyone that one equals one, eventually no one will be worth more than another, and every thing, idea, person will be interchangeable, as if pulled out of a deck of identical cards. We need to undermine any principle of authority between opinions, then, so that true and false are no longer distinguishable, no matter who expresses them. To do so, however, we need to take down the public figures that hold a moral or scientific authority—that is, those who think they know more than others, the so-called experts.

Doctors? Servants to big pharmaceutical companies. Climate scientists? Irresponsible scaremongers. Statisticians and economists? Number meddlers bought by the elite. Writers? Armchair activists. In fact, being an "intellectual" or an "expert" needs to become inconvenient, as no one has really figured out what purpose they serve anyway. Do they know or understand more than others? If they are truly democratic, they should be ashamed of having even started to think that. In this complete nullification of competences and experience, everyone will ultimately be able to talk without anyone really listening. The result will be that whoever controls the new media will still be the ones in control of the old media, with the new advantage that everyone will be convinced they are expressing themselves, rather than being silenced. Being able to dissent may be democratic, but dissent by itself fortunately does not create democracy if it doesn't effect change.

Social media hides another type of potential, which will be extremely useful to the plotting of a fascist trajectory: it's a series of platforms, from which the head can speak directly to the people, bypassing the mediators who often distort the meaning of his message. No journalists paid by the opposition. No leading questions. No printed interviews (no one reads the papers anymore anyway). It's better to reach the people directly and informally, with a colloquial style like an "Ask the Head" advice column like we used to have in magazines.

This way, the head will give the impression of listening to all requests, even though he will be the one deciding what to reply to and what to ignore, as is right. Unfortunately, this does not mean that

journalists will disappear, or at least not immediately: they will be allowed to ask questions just like
everyone else, but this way their questions will count
as much as everyone else's, and if they receive no
answer, they'll just be more internet background
noise. The head's replies, on the other hand, will be
shared thousands of times, because it's not true that
we're all equal in new media: if you're a nobody,
you're equal to other nobodies, but if you use these
tools from a position of power, that same power will
be felt through them. All tools, if used in a fascist
manner, become useful to fascism.

One of the undeniable advantages of these tools is
that they are extremely efficient in communicating
short, clear and easily memorized messages. No
more inquiries, public explanations, long TV de-
bates or special newspaper investigations to understand what goes on behind the scenes: they only end
up creating more confusion.

Ordinary people, forced to take an interest and
engage in a democracy, will live blissfully under fascism, as they'll be able to tend to their own business
and will happily delegate everything else to the head.
For this reason, trying to get them to understand

the details of what is happening is a waste of time: it is sufficient to give the necessary information to allow them to rely on those making the decisions. You don't even need to make sure that the information is always true, because truth in itself doesn't exist: it's a political detail, not a real one, and so those who rule politics also, and always, rule the truth.

Unlike in a democracy, the aim of fascist communication isn't to be understood, but to reiterate, so we're lucky to be fascists in the age of the internet: it's less effort, because the tools were designed specifically for this. What is sharing if not an infinite reiteration of a single message from a single source? By using a few keywords and simple slogans, maybe even making them into hashtags, eventually all the work that required an entire department will be voluntarily done by the people, with the added bonus that they will also believe themselves to be the source of the message, and not its recipients.

At this point, you might think that fascism needs to communicate through social media with simple messages, but you would be mistaken—as are many who believe in democracy. Complexity mustn't be simplified, it must be *trivialized*. Simplification, as well as being extremely difficult, means removing the superfluous and keeping the essential; but it's the superfluous that generates the useful white noise that makes all voices the same and neutralizes that pesky dissent.

What we must do instead is create multiple trivial messages. A wave of them. Trivialization removes the essential from the people—as it is the head's prerogative—and leaves them with the superfluous, allowing them to talk about anything except what isn't necessary for them to know in order to live happily. It's not that hard. For any given complex situation, there are at least twenty ideas about how to solve it, but there is usually only one, big fear. Finding that fear and making it the message is way more efficient than trying to simplify the twenty different solutions, which no one cares about anyway. People want their fear removed, not to debate possible solutions; fear is for everyone, solutions are for the head. If there is a general, diffused dissatisfaction and the head has yet to come up with a solution, the best strategic trivialization is to give the people an enemy to blame.

Making
enemies

Y ou can't become a fascist without an enemy, because for fascism to impose itself, it needs to oppose another. You may think that this is no different from a democracy since, after all, every time we vote it's someone against someone else. That's not entirely true, because supporters of democracy can't give up the idea of legitimizing differences of opinion and belief, and keep being inexplicably generous toward dissenters. Thus they don't call their political antagonist their *enemy*, but rather their *opponent*, a useles and annoying figure who despite differences of opinion still fits within the discourse of recognition—a bit like in martial arts, where, after having beaten each other up, you both have to bow.

In a democracy, no one takes away the opponent's opportunity to say what they think, organize it, even present it as a political program to receive approval. The opponent is someone who is even

expected to follow, at alternate periods, in the seat
of power, even though everyone hypocritically then
hopes that their opponent never actually succeeds.
The opponent in a democracy, however, remains a
pain even after a loss, because they become the opposition. You never get rid of them: they're always
there, watching your every step, highlighting your
mistakes, reminding everyone of your unkept promises and forcing you to act on your words. In any
other real-life situation, no one would keep someone
so annoying that close, and yet democracy allows
these kinds of people to sit in the very place where
decisions are made. It makes sense that some might
call it the worst form of government.

This tendency of democracies to legitimize everything is undoubtedly stupid, but extremely useful
for fascism: if you show up for an election having
cautiously avoided explicitly saying "We're fascists,"
there is a good probability that the democratic fools
will let you run, take votes and even rule, convinced
that you're just an opponent with different ideas. A
bit like Troy, there is no need to lay siege to it: you
just need to build a wooden horse, and democratic
institutions themselves will open the door for you.

Introducing yourself as the opponent is an excellent Trojan horse.

"But would progressive and conservative democrats really believe that we're not actually fascists?" you'll quite rightly be asking yourself. Of course, and the reason is obvious: they all wish, with all their might, that fascism didn't exist, that it's something from the past and that there is no chance of its reappearing. It follows that they will voluntarily ignore all signs that point to the fact that we've always been here, we never left, and we've been reorganizing for years. They'll call us "nostalgic," "alt-right," "nationalists," or whatever, but they will be the first not to want to say the word "fascists," because it reawakens not us—as we're fully awake—but their own ghosts.

If, in spite of all this, someone catches on, and speaks that name, with or without the "neo-" prefix, and has the gall to demand that we not be allowed to run in an election or to have headquarters, or even pursues legal action against us, that is when the *opponent* Trojan horse becomes fully functional. All we need to do is cry: "See? You don't actually believe in democracy! You want to silence dissent, crush differences, pluralism, opinions different from yours," and the impossible will happen: being a flawed mechanism, a democracy accused of being anti-democratic will short-circuit, and its supporters will even start thinking that they are the real fascists if they don't let you speak. This is the beauty of democracy: unlike fascism, it can always be used against itself.

Playing the opponent is useful to get into the system, but once inside you need to start acting honestly: there are no opponents, only enemies. There are no questions about an enemy: we're not talking about someone who is part of the system, but rather an anomaly, a tumor. Let the supporters of democracy refer to *opponents*, especially when referring to you, so that each time they name you they are delegitimizing the system itself. You, on the other hand, must start as soon as possible to call them what they are: your *enemy*.

This isn't hard. Unlike an opponent, with its annoying tendency to be recognizable in a person or faction, the enemy doesn't have a fixed identity, often not even a name, so it can be found in general, vague categories such as "migrants," "Islamists," "markets," "liberals," "activists," "globalists," "anarchists" or "feminists." This allows us to call absolutely anyone an enemy, even those who have no idea you exist. The advantage is that you can fight the enemy entirely from one side, because it will remain useful whatever the reaction: it just needs to exist (and, sometimes, not even that).

To make the shift from opponent to enemy more effective, we need to leave behind all the niceties of good sportsmanship that are part of a democratic system: the enemy deserves no respect, otherwise you can't obliterate them; if you always stop just before removing them, the process keeps repeating itself forever. To make sure people understand that the fascist lexicon isn't the same as that of a democratic time-waster, we must talk about the enemy as a deformed, even dehumanized entity; for example, comparing them to animals that share the negative aspects of humanity. There are many good word choices, such as *parasite, cow, worm, shark, bitch, vulture, pig, vermin, chimp, roach*. Even *sheep* will do, and depending on your circumstances, a generic *animal* is also pretty effective. If you choose not to use animal terms to refer to the enemy, you can use nicknames that diminish their actual name or highlight a physical defect, making use of a part for the whole. If they're short, call them a dwarf; if their name lends itself to it, play with its sound or meaning; and if they're black you can comment on their tan. In the case of public outrage, all you need to do is claim you were joking and that this type of language falls under rightful political or satirical commentary: in a democracy, they'll drop it. In the meantime, however, the messed-up name, that nickname, that physical defect will be on everyone's mind and what had previously been a respectable opponent will become the target of mockery, of disparagement, of hate. In other words, a true enemy.

The second step, after delegitimization, is blame. It's always hard to blame an opponent, as they have an individual personality and ideas and perform specific acts, and can therefore only be blamed for something they've actually done. An enemy, on the other hand, as they have no real identity, can be accused of absolutely anything, kickstarting the process of transitive responsibility: the faults of a single enemy can be applied to an entire category that they belong to. A black man rapes a woman? All black men are rapists. A Muslim steps into a crowded space crying to Allah? All followers of the Prophet are potential terrorists, even the Pakistani baker downstairs, who's never held anything in his hands but oven gloves. This moral shift must obviously not be effected in the case of good deeds, which, even when publicly recognized, must remain the exceptional actions of an individual.

Unlike supporters of democracy, we are not fools: there will be the need to specialize, in order to avoid having someone use these same rhetorical weapons against us. To do so, we must ensure that no generalization concerning us, unless positive, can be spread. People must always consider it a given that everyone like us is a good person until proven otherwise, and even in the case of someone picking up a gun and shooting at people in the street, not only are they not the rule, but they would have to be described as a lone wolf, a madman who cannot be held responsible for his actions—and as such, it becomes even less possible to shift his faults onto anyone else.

In this rhetorical game, a white man who rapes a woman will always and forever represent himself, while a black migrant will represent all black people and all migrants, too. To reinforce this building up of the enemy, it will be useful to start spreading the idea that the same crime is much worse when perpetrated by an outsider rather than one of us, confirming the notion that the enemy is never better than us, but rather worse than us in all possible ways. In any case, never our equal.

The enemy as described, then, is removed from any required debate. There is no more need to dissent or to bow politely at the end of a fight. The enemy needs to be destroyed and removed from society, with or without brute force. This level of disgust is hard to achieve in the confines of a politically correct democracy, but it can be done: we must constantly undermine the possibility of a dialogue with the category we have chosen as the enemy. For example, we must convince everyone that our culture and that of the enemy are irreconcilable, making it pointless to have a conversation. We can make the enemy a mystical hidden power, unreachable and poorly defined, always planning our demise, so that any attempt to compromise will be seen as an ominous trap. This strategy is better served by conspiracy theories, as the unprovable enemy is easier to hate than the one you might meet every morning for coffee.

How do we choose the best category to represent the enemy? It must always be represented as threatening, because no one can be an enemy of someone who lacks the strength even to stand upright. The challenge is that many of the useful enemies of fascism don't seem threatening. They are. Migrants coming in boats from Africa and the Middle East are a threat, but we need to contextualize it. Some are fleeing wars and famine with pregnant women and small children, but there are always strong, young men among them, full of hope and therefore potential competition in the fields of work and women. They come from cultures and religions that, if they took hold here, would force us to face our differences. The images that show them as victims are deceptive, and lead to the creation of a type of mercy that we can't afford people to feel.

There is only one way to make something so fragile into a threat: make ourselves even more fragile, and pit the two fragilities against each other. They're looking for work? We don't have any to begin with. They want to build their places of worship? In their countries, people of our religion are persecuted and killed! They're fleeing a war? Our elderly come first, our young people seeking opportunities abroad, our families on the brink of poverty. If the game becomes executioner versus victim, it is already lost: no one wants to be the bastard slamming the door in the face of the hungry. If, on the other hand, we're *all* victims, then our fragility makes us equal and no one has any obligations toward anyone else. This is why we need to talk about ourselves as a little weakened, united but fragile, worn out and abandoned, alone against the world (Europe, the markets, foreign powers, anything goes), and victims of an imposed disease that hinders otherwise certain economic development. Until fascism is fully established, there will always be someone trying to claim that people coming from the outside have a greater claim to victimhood than those inside; against this type of rhetoric, we must pull no punches, and respond with direct, delegitimizing attacks.

Virtue signalers, defenders of human trafficking, armchair activists, women who only want a black lover.

The Pope? He can welcome them into the Vatican, but first he must look at the horrors and corruption already present in the Church.

You're crying for all the deaths at sea or in the Central American caravans? I've never seen you cry for our elderly who can't survive on social security alone.

NGOs? Accomplices of traffickers, working with

refugee programs, making a profit on the backs of these poor people.

The possibilities are endless, but the result is always the same: the more people feel victimized and under threat, the more united they will be in their own defense, and will look to a strong figurehead to guide and protect them.

Save us all

The world is a difficult place. We are surrounded by enemies both external and internal. Within our borders we have to keep fighting every day against unemployment, our best and brightest leaving the country, our salaries not lasting to the end of the month, cuts to our health and welfare systems, and education no longer ensuring a future for anyone. Outside, foreign markets can't wait for our companies to be begging for help, our artisans and workers wasting away in unemployment and seeking benefits.

Cultural threats are no less worrying. There's an entire world that can't wait to cross our borders to impose its backward customs, its bloody religion, its stinking cooking, and its strange way of looking at things. They want to change us, and to do so they exploit our solidarity. They come over here, asking for shelter, and with the excuse of wanting to be more like us they slowly make us more like them. It starts with eating kebabs and it ends with removing all religious imagery that might hurt their sensibilities, starving us of our proud roots and identities. They want to perform an ethnic substitution, and they make use of the fact that we're having fewer children—as if not having children were a choice, in this unstable modern world!—by sending over hundreds of young men, who start out poor and are only after some food and used clothing, but who will be less poor tomorrow, and will demand the same rights as us, our jobs, our women. They will demand to be us.

Fascism can protect us because, unlike democracy, it realizes that all of this is a threat. Supporters of democracy, even those who would never want be seen as lefties when it comes to the economy, are too close to the ideology of diversity, to reveling in the joy of diversity in the world, to learning from each other, to ethnic foods, to multiculturalism, to ecumenism, and so on, mixing things that have no reason to be mixed. Meanwhile, the world remains a difficult place; we're weaker by the day and our only hope is to defend ourselves with all that we have, relying on those who can guide us against the ongoing assault. This scenario may seem to many like an overreaction, but better to preempt and prepare for our demise than to be surprised by it.

Democracy, always naively trusting of progress and the positive potential of humanity, is the least suitable instrument to face all this, especially as most democratic constitutions are based precisely on those values that stand in the way of recognizing these threats for what they are: equality, solidarity, human rights. Democracies are not predisposed to recognize the fact that human beings, except for those with whom we share blood and soil, are a threat. The mantra "stay human" that so many bleeding-heart democracies love ignores the fact that we humans are the dominant species on the planet precisely because we hunt everything else. Staying human, in the natural world, means surviving, putting ourselves first, before anything else, being able to defend ourselves against everyone and, if necessary, against our own kin, too. We fascists, then, also say "stay human," but the way in which we say it is based on the natural sciences, not the feelings of those who have already paid off their mortgages. Fascism must make everyone understand that in dangerous situations (i.e., always), it can, much more effectively than democracy, defend the weak or those who feel they are under threat. Of course, there are also those who are weak and don't know it. All we need to do is find a way of showing them that they are.

It's not a difficult task, really. In our late-capitalist society, only 1 percent of the population can't be defined as weak, as they earn too much to have any weaknesses. Everyone else has something to lose, and if you show them that it's under threat, they will trust whoever proves to be able to defend it.

The first priority, the one for which we all work and fight, is always family. Highlighting how weak families truly are is therefore crucial in order to rouse the fighting spirit of fathers and mothers. The enemies of a family are those who try to undermine the natural roles of man and woman, or their traditional functions. The two groups who attempt to do so, and have done for decades, are always the same: feminists and gays.

During the years in which democracy thought itself invincible, to the point that all possible deviant ideologies have been forced upon us, the idea was established that feminist causes—abortion, divorce, gender equality, sexual emancipation—were to be praised and supported as a form of progress. In the same way, we've convinced a large part of society that the wishes of the gays—no discrimination, marriage and even adoption—are actual human rights. Neither is true; both are dangerous. The supposed emancipation of women has only led to fewer births and increased competition with men in the workplace, leaving at home empty cribs, cold dinners, and mounds of unwashed laundry. The so-called sexual revolution has only created more confusion and has taken women away from men, to the point where we can no longer even compliment or touch a woman without immediate allegations of assault. On the flipside, while women no longer want to marry or take care of a family, gays demand to be able to do so as if it were normal. This is the topsy-turvy world of democracy, where every mockery of society is justified just because a majority decides it is so. But nature cannot be subverted by imposing laws, just like the sun won't set in the east just because a majority vote for it. This mayhem destroying the notion of the natural family finds its roots in the impossible conviction that women are equal to men and gays are equal to heterosexual people.

Fascism, the politics of common sense, has as its main duty that of bringing things back to their natural order, and starting with women is crucial, because woman is the support of man, and man is the head of the family: if you remove her, it all falls down. Fascism knows that women aren't independent. In nature, the female seeks protection, and it's no different for human females: they need men because the latter are strong, and they are weak. They are precious thanks to their maternal functions and naturally inclined to warmth; women are delicate and it is our duty to protect them, especially when—in their irrationality—they claim they don't need to be protected. They must never be exposed to risks, find themselves in places that aren't safe, or behave without inhibition, making others think they may be available, putting them in danger. The world out there is full of men from other cultures who are ready to rape them, as they consider them inferior objects.

Fascist wisdom must remind women that their demand to be strong is precisely what made them into targets, and that removing themselves from their naturally assigned role has also destabilized their men, who often—wounded and feeling abandoned—react in a disorderly way, with consequences that it would be best for all to avoid. Women's shelters are a useless by-product of feminism, as they encourage women to accuse their partners of criminal acts, rather than solving such conflicts at home and keep-ing families together. A fascist government's pro-posal, therefore, would include policies supporting not women *per se*, as she is not a social subject to be considered autonomously, but rather mothers and their function. The solution would be to identify the category of "mother" among the various political identities. Such an explicit choice of language, how-ever, might be counterproductive among those cor-ners of democracy that still subscribe to old-school feminism. Once these are weakened, mothers will finally be back at the center of family life, and with it, politics.

As for gays, it's not even worth explaining the threat that their mere existence poses to the human race. To remove them or cure them, after so many years of democratic passivity that has infected so many other countries, would require a disproportionate amount of effort and money. Forcing them to hide so they can't be bad role models for our young, how-ever, is a duty that cannot be ignored. Any attempt to normalize homosexuality is a threat to families and the continuation of our species. Children must be protected against the gay agenda—which uses the excuse of removing discrimination to make them believe they can be who they want to be, rather than teaching them to want to be what they already are—as much as from gender equality. Boys will be boys, and girls will be girls.

It is crucial to talk about the fragility of a long-forgotten group, one that most of all should and will represent the majority in any Western society: the elderly. Most live on meager incomes and no one really takes care of them. Solving the current issues with the social security system is unfortunately impossible due to super-democratic gender equality, which has allowed women to work, taking away their time and willingness to have and raise children who would pay taxes to care for older generations. Women have put themselves before the needs of the community, and now all of society has to pay the price. Retirees in rural areas might still have some difficulties in understanding that the consequences of the failures of democracy cannot be the burden of fascism. What they can understand, however, is a stall in their town square giving out bags of food, because if you can't solve the root cause of a social illness, you can make a show of solving the symptoms as they flare up. Unfortunately, a caring gesture alone toward a destitute old man or woman will not make him or her a fascist: it's necessary to clarify that solidarity and politics are not the same thing; fascism, even when it's handing out food, is never not-for-profit—fascism is always political.

While offering solidarity to the marginalized we must therefore insist and remind everyone that we're not doing so for the marginalized in general, but for *our* marginalized: ours come first and then, if anything is left over, other people's marginalized. And we all know there is never anything left over. Each time the elderly receive a single bag of supplies from us fascists, they must be reminded that democracy is probably handing out two more to a foreigner. Each time supporters of democracy try claiming we need to help the weaker members of society, fascism must remind them that the first weak are our own, and that neocolonial democratic policies have abandoned them, preferring people who don't belong with us. In this way, we will make clear that our enemies are both those people who demand to be helped without deserving it, and democracy itself, as it affirms that being helped is a universal right. The weakness of our own will be our strength.

For many, this focus of fascism on social issues may seem paternalistic, but if paternalism means the

caring gaze of a father watching over everyone, especially those who can't cope on their own, then
we'll gladly take it. A state is a family, where the
father is the head and behaves, rightly so, as such;
if a single person takes on the responsibility of rep-
resenting everyone, then that person must also look
after everyone. You were the first to be able to see
the margins in our society, therefore you have the
right to become their protector and gatekeeper.
Under fascism, everyone must feel safe. No one
must think that they are forced to become strong
and independent by their own means, because we
know that some weaknesses are structural and cannot be solved. Convincing people that it's possible
for them to become independent of the state demon-
strates a lack of responsibility toward them: it
makes them believe they no longer need protection,
so that when a real threat emerges, they won't be
ready to face it. The weakness of individuals is crucial to the strength of the state, because those who
recognize their own weakness rely on the strong.
And the strong, when necessary, don't back down
from defending their own.

When in doubt, strike

Multiple contradictions run through the veins of democracy, and all can be exploited by fascism. The biggest of them all, however, is non-violence. I know this might appear counterintuitive, but even though it's a form of government founded on a conflict of positions, democracy still insists on rejecting violence as a way of doing politics, which makes as much sense as training tarantulas by only feeding them lettuce. According to the flaccid democratic spirit, any demonstration of dissent, if there is one, must be respectful, regulated, organized, and mediated, all adjectives that better suit a middle-aged tea party than an expression of disagreement.

Fortunately, we are human beings, and our coexistence itself generates the conditions for violence. This means that even democracies are forced to develop types of hypocrisy in their own administration, first of all when it comes to the legitimization

of violence: it is legal only for law enforcement acting on behalf of the government and its branches.
Effectively, as with tobacco and alcohol, violence is
a state monopoly when it comes to a democracy.
Treating it like a drug, however, has the paradoxi-
cal side effect that even the government that makes
use of it can feel guilty about it, as if they were taking a swig in secret, always apologizing and cordon-
ing it off with so many restrictions and so much
tape that resorting to it can be worse for the officer
than the criminal who deserves it.

The result of this guilt is that, as absurd as it may
seem, in a democracy you cannot beat up someone
caught committing a crime. If they have information that they're not willing to share, you can't ex-
tract it from them. If they refuse to confess, it's
extremely difficult to make them cooperate through
force, especially in the more degenerate democracies, the ones where torture has been banned. In
those countries, if you were to catch a pedophile
molesting a child and you want to find out if there
are any accomplices, your hands are tied: you can't
use electricity, or sharp instruments, or blunt ones
either; there's no way you can threaten their family,
and psychological pressure is only allowed up to a
certain point; if democratic extremists always had

their way, leaving the perp tied up and naked in a room, in the company of a single mosquito, would be enough to get Amnesty International involved.

In those fortunate countries where torture isn't a crime, we can still use violence—with caution, still being careful about not being seen and making doubly sure that there are no casualties, which would risk a moral and legal trial, especially when the crimes are related to political dissent. And so we arrive at the biggest paradox of them all: if a police officer kills a political protester, they'll end up in jail and will never be a police officer again; if, on the other hand, a protester kills the police officer, sure, they'll go to jail, but they'll also go back to protesting, because in a democracy you can never take away the right to dissent. I feel for law enforcement forced to act within such an irrational system: as representatives of the state, they can make use of violence, but then the state itself demands they act kindly while doing so. It's a total paradox, but actually quite useful for us: what better soil than their own resentment in which to grow positive feelings toward the fascist method?

Fascism, you see, would never place anyone in the contradictory position of non-violence, especially not someone in law enforcement: the use of violence as a consequence of necessity isn't just allowed, it is heartily recommended. Our organizational model (and therefore our political one) is that of natural order, and in nature violence is boundless, without any moral judgment. The wolf guts the lamb, but do we put the wolf on trial? The alpha lioness kills the cubs of her predecessor, but will we ever condemn her for that blood? Elephants charge and trample whoever invades their turf, but no one considers them criminals for this violence. Instinct is what guides violence, necessity—these are the primordial forces of our nature as the dominant species.

Domination is violence in itself—and this may shock the pure souls of democracy—but the alternative is to be dominated, because in a violent world you can't choose violence: it already exists. The only thing you can choose is to enact it or receive it. We fascists solved this quandary a long time ago. If the weak spot of democracy is the damning conviction that violence is the last resort of the incompetent, we believe the exact opposite: non-violence is the refuge of those incompetent enough not to see that violence can be necessary. If you have an enemy, you have to be ready to do anything to take

them down. If you have a head, you have to be ready
to do anything to follow him. If you hold something
or someone dear, you have to be ready to defend
them by any means necessary. There are no compromises when you love your country, your coun-
trymen, your family, your culture, your faith, as if
they were the only ones in this world—a world, as
many tend to forget, that only respects what it fears.

Fascism, however, never forgets this and always en-
courages intimidatory violence in all of its forms,
from the range of methods and circumstances available to the state, to the reasonable force of the individual. In the latter case especially, the legitimacy
of violence is both practical and didactic. Weapons
in the hands of the people will never be important
during the moment in which a fascist state is born.
The head will offer a sufficient guarantee to reas-
sure everyone that, if brute force is needed, his will
be enough. The more the head expresses his promise of violence, the less the people will feel it necessary to do it themselves, feeling safe and protected.
Individual weapons, however, are necessary in the
first phase of fascism, when coexistence with the
weakness and passivity of democracy will allow

the idea to take hold that the state isn't doing enough to protect its people. In that yet unripe circumstance, life itself will act as an accomplice to fascism: for every grisly case in the news, for every instance of trespass, every rape, every theft, we will be able to clamor for laws that allow us to use reasonable force in our own homes, to reinforce the idea that the democratic state isn't doing enough to keep us safe, forcing people to do it themselves. Once the strongman arrives in power, the guns will be lowered, but for that to happen, they must first be raised. The head will always have the assurance that if people have been willing to pick up weapons for him, they will be ready to do so again if need be.

Talk of weapons, however, is already a late-stage fascism topic. The spark for the assertion of necessary violence starts much earlier: language. A fascist must always tell it like it is from the start. In order for violence to come back as an instrument of political struggle, it is crucial to abandon all linguistic half-measures and call a spade a spade. This is particularly necessary when talking about the disadvantage of initial coexistence with democracy, which constantly attempts to change the names of things.

In this set of circumstances, as fascists, we must at least demand from our own words that blacks stop being "people of color" and revert to being blacks. Whores are not "sex workers," cripples are not "differently abled," the unnatural conditions of deviants mustn't be blurred into the incomprehensible LGBT etc. acronym, and any obstacle mustn't be sweetened by calling it an "inconvenience," because it is, indeed, a fucking obstacle.

Supporters of democracy will react with shock, because this will crash their hypocritical framework, but you must always—no matter if you're speaking at a rally, into a journalist's microphone, in the pages of a newspaper, or from a seat of power—call upon the right to freedom of expression, to political criticism or satire. Insist that what you're doing is only a "provocation," an expression that a democracy takes to mean that you're doing nothing tangible, while you're still actually doing what the word means: provoking violent thoughts so that they may lead to action.

Political correctness has killed the fresh directness of our countries, forcing us all to pretend not to see what is right in front of us. For the sake of appearing kind we've become liars, accepting

expressions that were supposed to make us look
better than people sitting in pubs and bars. Fascist
politics, however, has no need for fake intellectual-
ism in order to feel superior to those it represents:
we are not above the people, we are the people, and
we talk like the people. If there is one place in the
world where everyone can understand us, that place
is the pub, it's the bar, where you'll always find
more people than in a university, for sure. Fascist
language, if you think about it, is more democratic
than political correctness, because it never makes
anyone feel inferior, even though many supporters
of democracy will feel superior to it anyway. Don't
take it personally, but rather thank them, at least to
begin with. Every time one of them demands the
use of politically correct idioms or diplomatic speech,
maybe calling us unrefined or ignorant, they'll be
handing us the chance to show to the people that democracy is more concerned with filling their mouths
with the right pronouns than with enough bread to
eat. Let them do it: this is the only way for armchair
activists to learn that there is no society in a world
that prioritizes pronouns.

The going gets tough when we shift away from ordinary political discourse into the next stage: verbal

violence directed at the enemy. If internal annoyances should be dealt with by employing an already liberated vocabulary, the real enemy must be faced with performative words, ones that announce and prepare actions.

It won't be enough to insult them, calling them stupid or thieves or cowards: it is crucial to point out what is the right thing to do to delegitimize, eliminate, and erase them, because if you are able to say what you'd do to them, you're already halfway to doing it. For this reason, the words to use against them must be explicit. It will take some effort initially, as during the first phase—still unfortunately democratic—there could be some legal repercussions about hate speech or some such thing invented by democracy to protect itself. This is not a good reason to desist: when threats become apparent, that's when you see who truly has the balls to take action, and who prefers to bend to the arguments of diplomacy, in their tailor-made suits.

Fascism needs people with balls of steel, not gay pride-ready metrosexuals who at the very most can choose the color of the walls. The mouth of the head, always the prime mover of the people's behavior, must put forth calls to action, possibly in the imperative, such as *sink, pave over, fuck, forcefully remove*, *drain*, *grab*—any term that suggests the removal of the enemy from the common space is allowed, associating them with garbage, rubble, suggesting they are superfluous, forgettable. Those listening must understand that the wishy-washy liberal use of language is over; with fascism, problems will be called by their name, and solutions, where needed, will be drastic.

Voice of the
people

Not all populisms are fascisms, but every fascism is first of all a form of populism, because—though it is never born among the people—fascism talks about them in the way that the people like being talked about: strong-willed, weak only by circumstance, generators of national authenticity, the true heroes of society.

The glorification of the qualities of the people is the first step to eliciting a sincere fascist feeling in the masses. Everything that comes from the people is true and genuine, and even when presented a little haphazardly it must be embraced and supported as an expression of the national spirit. Fascism, however, must ensure that the distinction between populism and being only popular is always clear. Where populism means that everyone looks up to the head, democratic popularity allows everyone to look to each other, losing sight of the horizon. Democracy is popular because it develops among the ruling classes the feeling of being of the people, and among the people the feeling of becoming the ruling class, as if in a family the roles of father and child were interchangeable. This reciprocal behavior blinds us, because no one truly respects their peers. If you place your nose against a canvas, you will never glean its full beauty; you will never be able to speak of what you really saw. Populism is the opposite of popularity, as it always maintains the distance between the needs of the popular masses and the strength of those who can provide. The popular recognize themselves in the people, the populist can do more: offer to the people someone they can recognize themselves in.

It isn't hard to be populist as a fascist: it's the same as wooing the girl who knows she is ugly because every other boy has dissed her so far, and she is waiting for the one to arrive who will tell her that all the others have been idiots to ignore her beauty. That boy, with the right words, will be able to have her every time he wants and she will always happily consent. Have you ever noticed that pussy isn't democratic either? Not everyone has a chance, only those who go for it. And so, if you want to be a

fascist, be a charmer first: look around and find society's ugly ducklings. They're everywhere.

Consider, for example, all those who haven't been
able to study, for whatever reason. With the democratic fetishes of public education and literacy
schemes, we've convinced ourselves that everyone
must study—even though some might not want
to—just because an education is seen as a sign of
virtue. The result has been that those who never
wanted to haven't, have dropped out as soon as they
have been able to, and have been mocked for it for
years. Turn to them, to the poorly educated, who
keep being mocked, every single day, by those who
have studied even one day more than them. Tell
them that it's not true that an education is necessary
to succeed in life, that what really matters is the
school of life, that graduates are better than no one
(and that they're only walking around with an ex-
pensive piece of paper, after all), and never forget to
remind them that a pair of hands toughened by
honest, hard work is worth more than buttocks
square from sitting at a desk all day. Those who
don't know will finally be able to stop being
ashamed of their ignorance and start disparaging

those who have studied and have looked down on them for decades.

Being a populist, precisely because of its parallels with wooing the ugly girl, works best on women. Feminists have told them that they keep being treated as inferior to men, and should rebel against this subjugated position—all you have to do is show them that there is no subjugation to start with! Invoke their grandmothers and call them matriarchs. Remind them of the smells of their childhood, when a woman always stayed at home to prepare food. Remind them of the wisdom of household remedies, of homemade things, of mothers supporting their country with the gift of their love. Tell them that not only do ironing shirts and looking after children and the elderly not make them inferior, but they actually make them unique, gifted with the feminine intuition that a man will never be able to comprehend.

Announce policies that will favor such activities, such as tax breaks for those who stay at home to care for the elderly, and maternity bonuses for those who decide to have children. Tell women that they are better, and they—for the sake of feeling special again—will choose to do again what they had de-

cided not to do any longer, even when faced with
the possibility of doing something different: they'll
iron instead of study, they'll have children instead
of a career, they'll marry instead of claim their in-
dependence. If her man finds a way to make her feel
special, no woman will ever feel the need to be his
equal.

The category of being "special" is peak populism:
each time you find yourself in the presence of any
form of weakness, call it something special, promise to protect it, and those who have it will cease
asking you to change their situation. Are you
headed to the cities? Praise their productivity and
rigor, praise the small businesses that have made
our country great, oppose this to the leeching,
scrounging rural areas and promise to lower taxes.
Are you headed to the suburbs, to the countryside?
Invoke the sacrifices honest laborers make for their
families, praise the honesty of their work, their
ability to make do, their hospitality as opposed to
the coldness of city life, and promise renovations
and benefits. Rural areas? All special folk. Border
areas? Super-special. Islanders? Unique in the world.
Urbanites? No one else like them.

For each of these specialities there is a different

promise that a fascist must make. Supporters of democracy—intoxicated by their equality nightmare—would make the same for all, but the fascist knows that it's better to differentiate, because each social group has to imagine itself to be unique in the eyes of the head. Some statements might seem contradictory—the rural areas might hear that in the cities you're calling them lazy—but this doesn't matter in politics, just as it doesn't matter in courtship. No woman, except the queen from "Snow White," wants to be the fairest: all they want is to be desired when their turn comes.

The ability of the head to contain each of these identities and to make them feel represented is also seen in his appearance, which must always be populist. When he's talking to those who can't make ends meet, the head will wear jeans, hoodies: simple, cheap clothes. With the man of the house, he should instead show up in a shirt, smart but casual, letting them see the strength of someone who is self-made, even through all the formalities. With the powerful and professionals there will be a tie, of course, but the attitude will be fresh, young, ready to break protocol, because the energy of fascism is an impatient force and it only follows the rules until it can change them.

Once fascism is well established, the outfits will become secondary and it'll be the head's body that will speak to the country, maybe through challenges that require physical strength, stamina, and control, such as long-distance swimming in the sea, diving into ice-cold lakes, flaunting a happy, healthy sex life, or running marathons. The apex of populism is showing oneself in the bosom of one's family, maybe during a holiday, bringing strength back to the reliability of traditional values.

The real core of populism, the thing that allows it to be a cradle for fascism, is the universal theme of money. In a democracy, the discrepancy among the amounts of money possessed by different groups of people is the cause of many a problem: it clashes with the notion of equality (which nullifies merit) and the equally absurd notion of proportional contribution (as if earning more were a sin you have to atone for). Adhering to these two conditions is never possible in practice: both the rich and the poor will be unhappy in a democracy, as the former will feel persecuted by taxation and the latter forgotten about in all public services. For the populist fascist, fortunately, this distinction doesn't exist: we can have mass appeal only with the masses, but we can be populists with everyone, because the fear of losing what we have—no matter how much we actually have—is the same for everyone. For this reason, whether we're dealing with the poor or the rich, the fascist populist must always refer to "us," siding and sympathizing with the condition of the audience, and acting accordingly.

If we're dealing with people who can't make ends meet, there is little sense in trying to talk about large-scale reforms: emergencies can't wait for long-term solutions, and sometimes not even medium-term ones. If you were to ask a good supporter of democracy, perhaps between their Pilates lesson and vegan cooking class, they would start citing the parable about it being better to teach a man to fish than to give him a fish. It's an interesting story, but to teach someone how to fish (i.e., giving them the means of emancipation) you need several years: in the meantime, they will have died of hunger, and the people want to eat now, and rightly so. To give them the fish directly only takes five minutes, and so promising immediate, tangible help to those in need is a duty of fascism. All policies that act on the here and now are commendable and recommended. It doesn't take much: all you need is some extra change at the end of the month or the removal of a hated tax, and it'll be clear that what we really care about are actual people. No reform will ever compete with extra money in your salary, and no revolutionary law will be welcomed as much as removing property taxes. Facts such as these, other than having an immediate effect on those on the receiving end, also reinforce the idea of the head as a protector of those in need, and contribute to the creation of a population that relies more and more on him as a good head of a family.

Populism, when being adapted for the middle class, is a little different. Even though this group might be comfortable economically, and might even be able to put aside some savings, it is still very much aware of the fact that stepping down the social ladder doesn't take much at all, and it doesn't take much before you find yourself destitute overnight. Fortunately, the lower middle class are easy to please, as their dreams are as middle-of-the-road as they are. They'll happily tune in to talk about investments, as they can afford to do so and their preference is for property. All policies that allow the expansion of a property or that promise tax breaks on the sale and purchase of a house are a sure way to win the favor of this social category. The more the average income increases, the more the populist promises inflate like a soufflé and reach the heart of the interests of the upper middle class: taxes. If, as fascists, you can guarantee that higher incomes will not be guillotined (e.g., by offering a flat tax), the middle classes will be forever on your side.

Finally, we reach the populism specifically directed at the wealthy, those with whom not even the most generous of the supporters of democracy could ever be popular. These people are not many compared to the rest of the population, but they are truly wealthy and often occupy crucial structural roles: it's stupid to have them as enemies, and having them as friends is convenient for both us and them. Their financial well-being is derived not from their incomes but from accumulated wealth, and so their worries revolve around its protection and growth, because at this level inert capital is already a loss of capital. A populist must treat these people as if they were destitute, because when it comes to protecting their interests, even millionaires behave like the middle class. It might seem like a paradox, but this group is the one most interested in reforms, as it has no urgent needs and can easily wait for their effects. Populism for the rich, therefore, can entail promises of fiscal protection for offshore accounts, though this may also alienate the lower classes, who might feel swindled. It is much better to promise radical reforms that touch the deep structure of the state, such as contractual reforms that will lower the cost of labor, and plans to reshuffle retirement vehicles, removing the requirements of the employer toward its employees.

A real populist deals with everyone according to their needs: the poor receive some free fish every year; the middle class receive a fridge to store what's left over; and the upper classes receive the pond where everyone will have to pay to fish.

In all this, the head will be able to lead by example, by showing the people two different aspects of himself: if he is wealthy from his own labor, there is no reason whatsoever to deprive himself of the standard of living that such wealth allows him; in fact, that wealth marks him as a self-made man, and someone we can trust. He must, however, show himself to be generous with his wealth, funding many different organizations and making a show of being philanthropic. The other, more difficult path, is not partaking of the perks that are rightly his as head, sacrificing any public aid that might be seen as superfluous by the people. All fascists can and should make symbolic gestures that will let simple people understand that we are just like them: you will be able to see the effectiveness of this for yourselves if, for example, after years of official state cars, you use public transport or eco-friendly bikes, or walk instead.

This way, you will have played a good hand in marking your difference from the supporters of democracy. Economic populism isn't just constructive: it also helps the destruction of political enemies. In the case of people who question the head's measures, it will suffice to call them out as privileged snobs, unable to understand the needs of the people, because of their city houses, their jewelry and clothing, their property that no one on an average income would be able to afford—and they don't even know the cost of a quart of milk.

Associating the social status of an enemy with their trustworthiness is crucial: the people must believe that the more wealth supporters of democracy hold, the less of a right they have to represent them—by definition, the masses have no wealth, after all. These are the moments when—as a fascist—I am grateful to democracy: in a society that has promised everyone the chance to pursue well-being, anyone who feels they haven't achieved it will be resentful and frustrated, and these feelings can easily be turned into political tools. If you're brought to court, don't defend yourself on the topic: point out that those opposing you have it easy, as they have something to fall back on. Every time someone criticizes you, reply that it's easy for them to talk, with their cushy homes in the city, when real life is something very different. Boats, fancy cars, or pricey houses—especially if they can be suspected of having been acquired using politicians' salaries— are perfect weak spots to undermine any financially stable democracy supporter, and not because of their stability, but precisely because of their support for democracy. They were the ones to come up with the fetish for equality and so they are expected to live equally to the people. Democracy applied to the economy is an idiotic system in which everyone believes that only those who can't make ends meet understand those who can't make ends meet. You let them happily think that: the construction of fascist consent takes entirely different paths.

You will find unsuspecting, unexpected allies for
the application of populism among armchair activists (i.e., the democratic middle classes, especially
left-leaning ones). These are people—not necessarily wealthy, but always certain of their cultural
superiority—who feel the moral imperative to fight
social injustices in a capitalist society, but are also
aware that the latter is the cause of their well-being
or their hope of reaching it. What will they do?
Easy: to atone for their guilt, they will engage in
secondary fights, never those that matter. They will
throw themselves into them, because the radical
though unnecessary nature of their *activism* is what
dictates their shabby-chic *armchair* reality. And so
they will invest their civic passion in consequences,
never in causes. They'll march on every street for
this or that right to be recognized for the queers, and
they'll chain themselves up to protest against vivi-
section of the poor baby animals, or against frack-
ing, or the new road that will ruin the view from
their window, but they will never do the same against
a labor reform or a flat tax that will protect their
higher incomes.

Armchair activists, in other words, will never lift
a finger against the establishment of economic fac-

tors on which their socioeconomic status depends. The difference between them and a right-leaning democratic middle class is that the latter may very well use the same *armchairs*, but they will definitely not be *activists*, as they feel no moral need to join any fight. It's the same social category, but not the same ideology, because the right-wing middle class never really believed in this whole equality thing. As fascists, you will often encounter both; don't be surprised at seeing them being friendly with one another, the wealthy or cultured of either side of the middle class. Between courses of a shared meal, the lefties will think that the right has some fine people too, if we overlook their delusion of a right-wing ideology, while the right-wingers will regard the civil struggles of those sharing their meal the way you regard obsessions, tics, or personal quirks. Both middle-class groups will be useful to fascism: they will both let you carry on with your work, the one because they are in denial about the whole thing, the other because they are uninterested in anything that doesn't affect them.

In the end, however, only one will be truly complicit.

Lest we forget

The instructions that follow would have been better placed at the beginning, but I thought they would be better understood once the fascist method had been removed from any historical context, to clarify the point that anyone who wants to be a fascist can be, at any time, in any place, anywhere in the world.

It wouldn't be fair, however, to ignore the fact that we are fortunate enough to be fascists in a country that has inherited a legacy of imperial rule, one that can aid us in keeping alive the memory of what we have been—it is crucial to find pride in what we still are. This isn't easy in countries that (for now) still celebrate their part in historical anti-fascist struggles, as it means that history—as it has been taught—comes to us deformed, instrumentalized, and mystified. The effort to reclaim it, along with our imperial pride, will take some doing, which means we must start immediately. Every time you try touching their version, supporters of democracy rise against you, and it's easy to see why: they've told each other a story that makes them look really good and it's expected that no one wants to be told the opposite. They've been sly—maybe the only time they have been—in laying down some safeguards to their narrative: for years, in public education, we've been teaching children that the European resistance and the Allied forces were the heroes and the Nazi–fascists were traitors and willing accomplices in the horrors of a foreign power. This arrogant, violent behavior, which doesn't actually support their version, only goes to show that memory is a political object and memories of war are the most political: what and how to remember them is decided by the winners over the bodies of the losers, who are no longer able to tell their own story.

Things can change, though, because memory has the quality of fading: if it isn't preserved it risks disappearing, and this is the risk that supporters of democracy run each time a new generation is born and they forget to spoon-feed it their official but fake notions of history. It's already happening. For several decades now, they have felt safe in the knowledge that veterans and resistance fighters are still alive.

They have treated the fall of the Axis and its ideology as a fact so incredible that we need eyewitnesses to be able to believe in it. They thought the version of those who survived would be enough to demonstrate its truth. This is obviously not the case. Partisans, survivors, veterans do not own history, only their own memories, traces of a personal experience that barely belong to those who lived through it. True memory is a different beast: it's the way in which the dominant group of people chooses some recollection of the events from a specific time period, finds a productive way to use it, and passes it down as if it belonged to everyone.

Democracy supporters made a choice and called it history, but it's still a choice they made. For this reason, we need to clarify the distinction between memories and memory: the former are the personal belonging of individuals; the latter is the result of a collective process. The difference, for a fascist, is crucial: the keepers of memories will eventually die out, so it makes no sense to fight them directly. We just need to wait and prepare to reclaim the truth of our own past. The sequence that a fascist will follow, once the time is right, is linear: pollute the memory of others, then destabilize it and, finally, rewrite it.

———————

Polluting a false memory is the first step toward purifying it. Supporters of democracy have gifted themselves holidays that mark the triumph over fascism, such as D-Day or Remembrance Day. We've seen them justify themselves by creating a pseudo-patriotic rhetoric that on the one hand celebrates the role of their own heroes and on the other unabashedly smears the other side, in a black-and-white game that allows no space for nuance. But it's through nuance that you will be able to start the pollution.

During this first phase, you must never deny any of the accusations directed toward our historical role models, who for some might even be grandfathers or great-grandfathers: it's still too early and it would raise too much unmanageable outrage. You must, instead, fake humility, limiting yourselves to integrating their version of history. Keep repeating that there was "a lot more going on, too." Democracy pits young brave men against violent murderers? Tell them that it's easy to judge in hindsight, but back then everything was so blurred that even Churchill praised Hitler's qualities as a state leader. The supporters of democracy commemorate their dead? You must also show up with your laurel wreaths, silently remembering that the days on which the anthem is played are days of national mourning, not a celebration, because all fallen lives matter. If believers in democracy recount all the horrors of fascism (and they will), don't contradict them: set out to remind everyone of how strong we were in quashing them. And most of all, point to roads, infrastructure, monuments in Europe, and say: "They did good things, too." Don't underestimate the teachable potential of those spaces: the fascist ones speak of greatness, of victory, of efficiency and fierceness, not much different from what the British Empire once was; meanwhile, democracy's contributions are terraced houses and traffic circles. All those listening and watching will start feeling the cracks in the narrative monolith of democracy, but the worst that can happen to you is that you'll be called *nostalgic*.

As soon as democracy lowers its guard and starts taking for granted that its version of history is the only one possible, it means the time to destabilize it has come. What are the signs? Several small details; first of all, teachers will start claiming that there's no time to teach the full history of the twentieth century.

All you need are two generations of kids who

haven't been subjected to the blight of critical thinking, and your path will be clear for you. You've already made people doubt that historical facts can't be taught from at least two perspectives, both true under certain conditions. The next step is to start saying that maybe those perspectives may not be as reliable as they think. Claim that fascism has never killed anyone; at most it exiled people. Remind people that the empire brought civilization to what would otherwise still be savage lands. If you see that no one reacts to this, push a little further: start doubting the existence of major war crimes, including the Holocaust. Question how it happened, the actual numbers.

Even if they have never reacted before, at this point supporters of democracy will cease calling you *nostalgic* and start labeling you *deniers* and *revisionists*. But things will have gone so far that it will be hard to figure out who is denying or revising what. We live in a time when sources of information have lost their authority and the reliability of information is close to zero for almost everyone (see the section on trivialization in "To simplify is too complex"). At that point, everyone will be able to defend their own truth on an equal footing, but thanks to your efforts, the younger generations born in the age of destabilization will have more tools than their predecessors to help them understand that history written by winners is not necessarily true.

This tweaking of memory is also necessary in order to defend ourselves from the annoying tendency of believers in democracy to make all faults into responsibilities. The fault or action may be particularly bad, but it belongs to the past: everyone has done something to be blamed for, but those actions end with the people who committed them, or we'll never get anywhere. Responsibility, on the other hand, is a never-ending loop, placing a mortgage on both present and future, and you'll never escape it.

In a democracy, each time you are handed the consequences of a disaster inherited from those who came before you, you must also take on its burden, as if you were the one to have caused it, and act as though you are the one who has to solve it. This way of life is impossible to maintain, and yet this is precisely how the democratic school of thought has taught our children for years: continually reminding them of something they cannot be blamed for. Let bygones be bygones. I don't care about what fascists did during their rule in Europe: *I* wasn't the one who killed six million Jews in concentration camps (if any of these numbers are even true, of course), and *I* never signed any law about racial segregation, or bombed London from the skies. Why should I feel responsible for them, then?

This distorted version of history is moral blackmail, made to make people who weren't even around at the time feel guilty. It's a way to prevent alternative ideas to democracy from defending themselves fairly in the present. Try saying that Jews control the world economy and Western politics, and you'll immediately be put on a par with concentration camps. Try claiming that it's not enough to be born in a country to make a Negro into a citizen and you'll be labeled a Hitler sympathizer. After all, if you were to use this same strategy, and dare to blame the grandchildren of Resistance fighters for the Soviet gulags, you'd immediately understand that none of them would be pleased to inherit the disgusting actions of their grandparents, while still insisting that our supposedly inherited horrors should be paid for. This is the rigged game that memory plays in a democracy: changing the misdeeds of their grandparents into personal sins to forget, and those of ours

into a collective responsibility to be remembered for
seven generations.

This is why rewriting memory must be the final step
in the reclamation process. Facts, distorted or made
up by the rhetoric of democratic resistance, must be
told anew according to a truer version, one that re-
turns fascism's good intentions, its ability to structure a country, and that recognizes the efficacy of
its politics. It will be time to recognize the worth
and value of fascist thought and action in civil society, to dedicate roads and monuments to its noble
fathers and loyal sons, and we will finally be able to
put up for debate the absurd existence of a thought
crime such as a Nazi–fascist apology, which—so
much for democracy—punishes and shames the
simple gesture of raising an arm as a sign of respect
for what we could have been.

At that point, we will have ceased to be painted
as harmless nostalgics and deranged deniers. It will
be normal for democracies to call us fascists or neo-
fascists. It will also be our triumph: we will have
brought back to everyone's mind a word that only a
few decades earlier had been associated with the
dead and the past, consigned to a dark side of history

along with our own empire, to a reality we thought would never come back.

We did come back.

We are here to stay.

And in the end, in history as in geography, those who stay win.

Fascistometer

Tick all the boxes that seem to be common sense, and calculate your total.

☐ Universal suffrage is overrated.

☐ We have no moral obligation to help everyone.

☐ The average voter's IQ is the same as that of a moderately intelligent twelve-year-old.

☐ I've had enough of party and minor-party politics.

☐ How can someone be in government without a degree?

☐ My education comes from the school of life.

☐ In this country, anyone can just say NO and stop any crucial work.

☐ Rape is worse if committed by someone seeking asylum.

☐ Boys should be boys, girls should be girls.

☐ Our country's people come first.

☐ You can't fill your belly with culture.

☐ No one can sort out this country.

☐ A woman, no matter how powerful, should always step aside for her man.

☐ There is a reason that Western culture has shaped the world.

☐ Do we really need another debate about this?

☐ The benefits for those in power are an intolerable privilege.

☐ They started out as national socialists.

☐ Easy for them to judge, when they live in a cushy house in a gated community.

☐ There is such a thing as a natural family.

☐ I don't remember all of this solidarity for our troops.

☐ The gay agenda is getting a bit out of hand.

☐ They need to understand that people are tired.

☐ Our Christian roots must be protected.

☐ These people don't know what working means—it's a cultural thing.

☐ They're stealing our jobs.

☐ Trade unions are for people who don't want to work.

☐ Feminism has taught women to hate men.

☐ The first thing to do is reduce the number of people in government.

☐ They don't actually believe that—they're just virtue-signaling.

☐ A country with no borders isn't a country.

☐ They're all the same.

☐ We should be helping them in their own countries.

☐ A civilized country can't grant the vote to people who just came down from trees.

☐ They're not refugees, they're economic migrants.

☐ If the state can't protect me, I'll have to do it myself.

☐ Affirmative action is offensive to minorities.

☐ That's reverse racism.

☐ There's no difference between left and right anymore.

☐ I have a right to voice my opinion.

☐ These people should not be allowed to vote.

☐ Journalists are all biased anyway.

☐ Our violence is necessary; theirs is part of their culture.

☐ I'm not a racist/homophobe, but...

☐ Think about our men and women fighting for our rights.

☐ The liberal elite, in their fancy suits, are always looking down on us.

☐ Our own graduates can't find jobs.

☐ No one's thinking of the birth-rate crisis.

- [ ] If we go over to their country, we're not allowed to do it.
- [ ] The violent leftists started it.
- [ ] Gender studies is ruining families.
- [ ] Do we really need the separation of powers?
- [ ] Party time is over.
- [ ] There are fine people on both sides.
- [ ] They don't respect our traditions.
- [ ] Don't come complaining when they force a burqa on you.
- [ ] Girls are asking for it, dressed like that.
- [ ] Actions speak louder than words.
- [ ] We should round them all up and ID them.
- [ ] They keep changing parties—how can we trust them?
- [ ] They're the first to steal.
- [ ] When we migrated, we already had a job lined up.
- [ ] This is a witch hunt.
- [ ] The system isn't working.
- [ ] I'd kick them out and raze it all to the ground.
- [ ] If you like them so much, why don't you help them yourself?

0 TO 15:
HOPEFUL

If your score sits in this bracket, your level of fascism is still embryonic, and you currently resemble more an angry democrat than a serene, well-formed fascist.

This book, however, was written with the notion in mind that we can *become* fascists, so don't lose hope: your inadequacy is your starting point. All fascists, after all, have started from more or less democratic positions, and you'll be surprised to learn that the road isn't as long as you might think. You can start with the basics, such as limiting the amount of attention you devote to different voices trying to explain what's happening, and focus on just one; this approach will reduce your confusion and anxiety and will favor the logic of relying on a head.

At the same time, feed your intolerance and your suspicions by getting used to considering as a threat all the differences that challenge your beliefs, be they social, cultural, religious, or sexual. Only read newspapers that support this vision and only listen to the opinions of those who defend it. Don't waste

time trying to debate with those who disagree:
rather, get used to mocking them, slowly leaving the
field of debate in favor of one of disgust and rejec-
tion. It can take just a couple of months of these simple changes to raise your score to the next level.

16 TO 25:
NEOPHYTE OR PROTO-FASCIST

If you got this score it means that you're at least partially aware of how effective the fascist method is, and how it can be used with satisfying results by anyone who isn't ideologically precluded from doing so. Unfortunately, you still seem to consider it only one of the options, meaning you're willing to tolerate pluralism and might even feel the need to defend it. Be careful, as a system that incentivizes the presence, organization, and expression of the widest plurality of positions inevitably leads to a democracy. It's not too late: you can still do a lot with even this low a score. Keep demanding that the principle of freedom of expression must apply to the fascist method too, just as to any political action, and convince one supporter of democracy every day to treat you with the utmost tolerance. This way, you will contribute to the realization of what Karl Popper theorized about an open society: "Unlimited tolerance must lead to the disappearance of tolerance. If we extend unlimited tolerance even to those who are intolerant, if we are not prepared to defend a tolerant society against the onslaught of the intolerant, then the tolerant

will be destroyed, and tolerance with them." For
this scenario to be fully realized, we need dozens of
people not fascist enough yet to affirm fascism as
the sole possible method, but not democratic enough
to organize against it. People like you.

You're still a while away from fully adopting fascism, but you're on the right path, as you have already come to question the fundamental tenets of democracy, that untouchable Moloch. The first of its dogmas, as you know, is that there must be a vote for everything, but not on those so-called values such as antifascism and antiracism, which exclude discrimination based on faith, political opinion, gender, and financial or physical situation. Fortunately, you don't seem to think that a constitution or declaration should include this dogma, and trying to have a stable document of sorts is an outdated idea, especially when it comes to the checks and balances between the different branches of power and involvement of the people. You can start from this belief, grow in your fascist awareness, and help those around you grow, too. A good way to increase your score is to focus on removing the power of dissent in both the political and the financial spheres.

On the political side, you must ask for more direct democracy involving individual citizens, but at the same time ask for diminished collective representation. This way, while still allowing everyone to take part, you're removing the possibility of lobbying parties, committees, assemblies, associations, and other hubs of interest that enact the organization of political dissent. On the financial side, you must support the abolition of collective agreement contracts and promote instead individual, merit-based contracts, rendering corporations and trade unions useless. Once fascism is fully established, more will form, but this time concerning the pursuit of personal interests and not to address problems in need of a solution. Until then, everyone will be reduced to personal struggles and needs, and will feel the urge to rely on a strong figurehead. They will also perceive difficult situations as threats, in which the limitations of democracy can be flouted in order to make space for new rules.

36 TO 50:
AWARE MILITANT

Your total score is high because you're at an advanced state of fascist awareness and you already see reality through its tools. You're a natural defender of the method and its developments, and you act openly against its vocal enemies. You intervene in every public sphere to identify, stigmatize, and eliminate them in front of everyone, and you share content that makes us understand who we need to defend ourselves from. You face off without filter or mediation against whoever tries fact-checking you, and though reducing the conflict to a personal attack is already part of your strategy, words are no longer your sole tool of militancy. If required, you can raise your hands as well as your voice and act where needed, each time claiming self-defense, adverse circumstances, or that they were asking for it.

Having reached this level of awareness, you should already know that each time you act this way, the divide between what is allowed in a democracy and what should be done keeps expanding. Don't stop here: each time you cross a line, you're helping to move it. You may pay for it directly in the moment, but after you another ten, another hundred, another thousand will cross it. Don't back down: there's a whole population behind you.

51 TO 65:
PATRIOT

If you got this score, it's a sign that this book had very little to teach you: you've renounced all democratic impositions; you're already a convinced fascist, and it's very likely that you're already a point of reference for others, less advanced or less motivated than you, who look up to you to gain inspiration and examples in their own formation process. You have a great responsibility, and you cannot let them down. You've gone beyond the mere necessity of attacking the enemies of the people, highlighting their weakness. If you position yourself in this bracket, you've probably learned that you can invent further necessities, on the same principle as the man who beats his woman every night—he might not know what for, but she definitely deserves it.

However, you must also be constructive and reassuring. Keep up your sense of belonging to our country and our culture, showing your interest in the traditional family, female intuition, and natural couples. If religious institutions praise you, show yourself devout and loyal to our roots; if they oppose us, treat them as you would any other enemy: go for

their interests and highlight their weaknesses. Talk
to the poor, but deal with the rich, because financial
power supports the wealth of our country, and the
latter must see you as a friend and defender. Nur-
ture in those who despair the hope of protection, in
those who support you the idea of guidance, and
in those who oppose you the certainty that they'll
be quashed by any means possible.

Be direct and clear in your positions: as long as
you do this in a democracy, you will force them to
concentrate their efforts on dealing with you, instead
of the country. Even if they form a coalition against
you, they will do so as your enemy; as such, and with
the conviction of opposing you, they will validate
you. Most of all, don't forget to pass on these teach-
ings. Build the consciousness of the younger generations, so that fascism will no longer have to face the
dangers of democracy and its degeneration.

DISCLAIMER

I know: right about now you'd like me to tell you—
in closing—that this has all been a provocation,
that it was all a fun game to try to change our point
of view, but that now the game is over and everything
goes back in its place, the fascists over there, us over
here, on the side of democracy. But no. The things
I've written, though not all of them and not always,
I have actually thought out loud at some point in
my life—the more cold, superficial, angry, ignorant
moments—even if just for one second; and I believe
everyone else has, too. I had no interest in writing
a book against fascists from the past or the present,
Italian or American, local or global. Who the fascists are today is something that is not necessary for
me to point out. Those who build walls, those who
only offer solidarity with their own, those who pit
people against each other in order to control both
sides, those who limit civil rights and liberties, those
who deny the right to free movement using the
weapon of the law and the alibi of responsibility—
these are today's fascists. The problem is being able

to pinpoint anyone who isn't even marginally complicit in the legitimization of fascism as a method. The risk we run is saying: if everything is fascism, then nothing is. This is not the case. Not everything is fascism, but fascism has the amazing property, without adequate vigilance, of contaminating absolutely anything and everything.

THANKS

Alessandro Giammei, prime mover of many choices, was once more the one to suggest that I needed to think about fascism as a method. Giacomo Papi and Michele Alberico have gifted me, on more than one occasion, their diagonal lucidity, helping me to focus better on the theme and the topics, as did Leonardo Caffo, with his militancy. The partisan talent of Marco Brinzi has helped me realize the political necessity of talking about it in public, and the frontier spirit of Veronica Cruciani opened up the first spaces for me to do so. My priceless dialectic school is daily political debate with Omar Onnis, Federica Serra Pala, and Luigi Cocco. Lastly, the spirited intuition of Daniele Luchetti suggested the name of this book. None of these seeds, however, would've borne fruit had they not found the soil of an unyielding democratic education—the work of Costanza Marongiu, my antifascist mother.